# Forgive Who?

Donald W Smith

*Forgive Who...?* ISBN: 978-0-692-13483-2 © 2018 by Donald W Smith

Unless otherwise indicated, all scripture references are taken from the King James Version of The Bible.

Scriptures marked NIV are taken from THE HOLY BIBLE, NEW INTERNATIONAL VERSION ®. Copyright© 1973, 1978, 1984, 2011 by Biblica, Inc.™. Used by permission of Zondervan.

Scriptures marked NLT are taken from the HOLY BIBLE, NEW LIVING TRANSLATION (NLT): Scriptures taken from the HOLY BIBLE, NEW LIVING TRANSLATION, Copyright© 1996, 2004, 2007 by Tyndale House Foundation. Used by permission of Tyndale House Publishers, Inc. Carol Stream, Illinois 60188. All rights reserved. Used by permission.

PRINTED IN THE UNITED STATES OF AMERICA

*Donald W Smith*

# Table of Contents

*Donald W Smith*

# Dedication

This book is dedicated to my parents, Earnest Smith Jr and Bertha Smith.

To my birth mother, Barbra Faye Smith, who I will always love and be thankful to have heard all the great stories about her life.

To my sons, Paul Edward Smith, Marcus Dewayne Smith and Earnest Smith III, sons of whom a father can be proud.

To my daughters, Dawn Keeley and Deneshia Manning. I deeply appreciate the ladies you have become.

To my sister, Cathy Jones, who I love immensely and appreciate.

To Mother Nora Jackson, for her undying love and friendship.

To my wonderful readers, thank you for pursuing.

# Acknowledgements

First and foremost, if it had not been for the love, commitment and encouragement I received from Benson Agbortogo, my life coach, this book would not have been possible. He is a man I found to be a person of integrity, exemplifying God's love through his business model. He cares deeply for me and stated that if I was not going to stay committed, he would end my contract. To him, I would like to say, Thank you! Needless to say, working with him was more than a "gym membership."

I also would like to thank Elder Andre William and Jacquelyn William for their steadfast and unmovable friendship. They were my first life coaches, and without a doubt, Mother Nora, too. She followed me until we both found a Church family, that accepted, loved and gave us opportunities beyond my expectations.

To my publisher, Paul Nyamweya, who I have a great deal of respect for. I have learned the flow of words and how to express my thoughts and feelings in a way that will not project condemnation and division, but communicate love, encouragement, healing and reconciliation; which was my goal.

To Derek A. Lang, my book cover designer. Thank you for a job well done. Thank you for catching the vision.

I would also like to thank Sue Bruce, my undying friend to the end. It was because of you I have rental property I could afford. With your help, I was able to rebuild my life.

To Cynthia McGee, for the article on male emasculation, that gave me answer to why I felt the way I did and why I could not seem to move forward. I am deeply thankful for the eye opener that brought a deeply felt freedom that I needed in my life.

# **Preface**

You may be *struggling* to forgive someone.

You may be making *excuses* as to why you are not ready to move on. That is the very reason this book was written.

I am no theologian, but someone crying out to you with a message of *faith* and *hope*; to *inspire* and *encourage* you to face what you may not have been willing to deal with.

"Making America Great Again" was the theme of President Donald J. Trump's candidacy, *before* he was elected to the highest office in the land. Needless to say, since the election, his presidency has been *filled* with turmoil.

Many individuals have taken *offence*. Many government officials have left his administration, expressing their *disdain* and *displeasure* through the news and on the internet. Many books have been written *claiming* to tell-it-all.

This book is a tell-all of the pain that I went through because of divorce and how I was able to *stand* through it all. I was able to learn the *importance* of forgiving someone in the midst of what turned out to be a season of on-the-job training.

At the time, I was *serving* as Pastor of Harvest Church. I was *married* to someone who was going through her own struggles. We were married for *over* seventeen years. I loved her immensely. She confessed never really loving me. How we were able to stay married for all those years, God only knows.

I look back today and realize how *blind* I was. What a *lesson* it was to learn. It is my *hope*, you will *find* the help you need, or are looking for, in the pages of this book. My goal is not to hurt anyone, especially the woman I once loved. I have prayed for healing to happen in her heart.

Forgiving someone is vitality important. It will be a sad day to stand before God with *unforgiveness* and *bitterness* in our hearts and think we are going to hear Him say to us, "Well done, thou good and faithful servant; enter into the joys of The Lord."

Many have convinced themselves that God will be fine with them holding on to hurt. That is far from the truth. Holding a grudge *against* someone because they hurt you is an issue you *need* to deal with before it festers into something you cannot recover from.

The Lord can *help* you.

If you are not a believer in Christ, that can *change* today. The Lord loves you and will help you to move *past* your hurt. Not understanding forgiveness will put you in *bondage*. It is my prayer that as you peruse this book you will *recover* from any pain.

Many have said these words to me, "You do not understand my hurt."

That is probably true. That is the very reason we should take *all* our disappointments and hurts to The Lord. He will *never* turn us away. He will *help* us and *establish* us.

Pain is a *gift* nobody wants.

*Forgive Who?*

If the pain of forgiving someone who has hurt you is *troubling* your heart, please know that God is *willing* to help you if you call upon Him. "Casting all your care upon Him; for He careth for you," (1 Peter 5:7).

#itspasttimetoforgive

Donald W Smith

# Introduction

*Have you considered how "late" it is getting?*

It is time to forgive and *move forward* with your life. I have learned over the years that Forgiveness is a "commodity" in The Body of Christ. What concerns me is knowing that so many believers are *struggling* with releasing themselves to forgive someone.

Forgiving someone who has hurt you can be the *beginning* of a new life for you. It is time to be *free* and not burdened down with the cares of this world. Freely *enjoy* the life God has to called you to live.

I have been married...*twice.*

Both marriages failed because of our *unwillingness* to forgive. When I think back to the pain we experienced and the setbacks we endured, it was the unforgiveness that drove a *wedge* between us. The *selfishness* in our hearts and the *unwillingness* to surrender our will to God; led to struggles in both marriages that could not be overcome.

In the pages of this book, I will be transparent.

I will share my heart with the hope that someone will bear witness to how God's Power can *transform* your situation. With God's help, you can be an *overcomer*, just like the book of Revelation teaches us. (See Revelation 2 and 3.)

My *first* marriage lasted for over twenty years. You would think, with that type of investment, two people should be able to make it and rise above *any* obstacle they were facing.

I admit, we did not have good counselors in our corner.

*Friends.*

*In-laws.*

*Church members.*

I never got married with the *intention* of getting a divorce. I do not think anyone with their right mind starts out that way.

My *second* marriage lasted 17 years. This time around, I figured I had gotten it right. It was my hope I would not go through another divorce. I intended to *complete* my days and my legacy with her by my side. However, it was after she asked me for a divorce *twice*, that I came to the realization that she *meant* it. She wanted *out* of the marriage. During the 18th year, we went through the divorce proceedings.

If hurt is not dealt with, *it will surface later in your life.*

Many people are *unhappy.* They go through life each day *hoping* for a change. Yet, that change *never* comes, because many are *not willing* to make an *investment* for change.

The following verse is very clear on what happens when we handle a matter and *trust God* for the outcome. "He that handleth a matter wisely shall find good: and whoso trusteth in the Lord, happy is he," (Proverbs 16:20).

Do *the right thing* in your marriage.

Forgive...*your husband*.

Forgive...*your wife*.

Forgive any *friends* and *family members* who may have *hurt* you. An unforgiving heart will surface in many forms. I have learned over the years, that if someone chooses not to forgive you, *it will always eventually manifest*.

The problem is, every human being has a *past*. If we do not deal with hurt from our past, it will eventually *catch up* with us. I would love to meet someone *without* a past; but we all know that is impossible to do unless you *divorce your past* and not your spouse.

Divorce continues to be an *epidemic* in our society and in the church. God *hates* divorce. (See Malachi 2:16.) At times, that *frightens* me; because I know one day I will stand before God to give an account of my life and how I spent it.

I can truly say, in my heart of hearts, that I have learned to forgive *quickly;* and I might add...*without requiring explanation*. In the parable of The Lost Son, the father forgave his son without requiring him to *defend* his actions. (Read Luke 15:11-32.)

# Chapter 1

# Without Explanation

*You cannot expect what you are unwilling to do.*

You should not expect to get *heaven's* pardon if you are not willing to look past some *earthly* offenses. "And when ye stand praying, forgive, if ye have ought against any: that your Father also Which is in heaven may forgive you your trespasses," (Mark 11:25).

In the parable of the prodigal son, the young man *demanded* his inheritance of his father. He was ready to leave home and *start living* the life he believed he could have. He felt he could get *more* out of life by living it *his* way. Many of us have the *same* desire.

In *career*.

In *marriage*.

Even in *singleness*.

We all *want* to achieve greatness. Yet, some of us fall flat on our face and end up in the hog pen of life, like the Prodigal Son. (See Luke 15: 11-23.)

There is a *reason* you have ended up where you are in life today. Hurt people *hurt each other*. Hurt *clouds our thinking*. We do not think *straight* anymore.

Many people are *hurting*.  Ask yourself how many friends you have that *struggle* with forgiving someone?  Many believers, and unbelievers alike, are going through life from pillar to post *looking* for results.

When a believer does not see any results in his life, he *wanders* from ministry to ministry, or from leader to leader, in *search* of the answer.

*Why am I not having any success in my marriage or in my relationships with others?*

I am thankful they are, at least, *seeking* for answers. However, the problem with many is they are looking in the *wrong* place.

Many factors affect your decisions, yet it is often the *pain* you are going through that is *making decisions* for you. That is why the cycle of pain never *stops* unless it is *addressed*.

When people *abandon* a church or a job *without* addressing and dealing with the root cause of their leaving, that underlying factor is carried over, *unresolved*, to their *next* church or job.  Instead of seeking God and making things right *before* leaving, many *take* the hurt with them.

## The Lenses of Pain & Brokenness

This same scenario plays out in marriage and in relationships.  Whatever remains unresolved *never repairs itself*.  Through the lenses of pain and brokenness, many are making a decision to become a part of someone's life.  They will *never* be happy because they never went back to *resolve* why they *left* their previous relationship in the first place.

How many believers and unbelievers are walking through life, having not forgiven their husband, wife, friends or even family members, because of an offense? Some believers are *harboring* unforgiveness toward their Pastor or leaders in their previous or even current church? If you would be *honest* with yourself, how many times have you *hurt* someone and *did not even realize it* until that person had the nerve to *speak up* and *tell you* about it.

## Who Has Been Hurt By You?

Many of us have said something to another without realizing how it *hurt them* or may have *damaged* them for life. The truth of the matter is, we have all done things we were not aware of, unless someone *alerted* us. I must admit, there are people in society who live *to hurt others*.

You may be wondering, "How does the prodigal son fit in to all of this?" *Keep reading!*

It is past time for many to be *truthful* with themselves. Please be clear, I am not saying *everyone* is harboring unforgiveness in their heart. Even if there was only *one* in The Body of Christ harboring unforgiveness in their heart, that is *one too many*. I think we can agree on that. How many have *left* churches after promising God they would *stay* and *support* the vision of the Pastor or The Board of Directors? (Smile.)

You have probably heard the story about what happens if you have *just one* bad apple in a barrel. I think we would all agree that one divorce is *one too many*.

When the prodigal son came to himself, he decided it was time to *go back home* to his father *and ask for Forgiveness*. It was not until he was down and out that he *realized* he needed restoration. He needed to be *reinstated* back to his *rightful* place in his father's house. How awesome would it be if a large number of divorced couples, estranged friends and family members, could find their way *back* to each other?

## Do Not Ignore The Underlying Reason

In some cases, that will never happen, because so many remarried too quickly; hoping to solve the problem of loneliness and a need for companionship; without addressing *the underlying reason* for their previously failed relationship.

If we would be honest with ourselves, we can acknowledge that we have had *undesirable* encounters with unbelievers and carnal believers, who know *nothing* of God and His ways.

Only with God's *Help* and *Power*, can you have the ability to *forgive* someone for the hurt you suffered at their hand. Forgiveness plays a huge part. God's Word alone will bring about the *real* change that needs to be at work in our hearts. Making a *commitment* to study and read His Word will produce *lasting* change. An *authentic* encounter with God always causes a *transformation*.

When the father *saw* his son, he knew from his demeanor that a *change* had occurred in his son's heart. The rags he wore may have revealed he had hit rock bottom, however there must have been something about his appearance that revealed his change of heart. He was *ready* to be restored.

Since that was all his son desired, he received *Forgiveness without explanation.* The father was ready to *celebrate* and *reinstate* him. Even as the son stood there repenting, the father called for the servants to get a robe and shoes for him, and even a ring for his finger.

When someone asks you to forgive them, and you find yourself struggling with it, *ask God to help you.* The hurt may run *deep.* That is why you need to go deeper. God's Power and Love will help you get to that place and be healed. There will be more on the prodigal son in the next chapter.

## It Is Time To Make A Decision

Do you know someone who is *struggling* with Forgiveness and letting go of hurt? *Maybe that person is you.*

It is time to *make a decision* to forgive.

*Your pain was in making the decision not to forgive whoever hurt you.*

It is my goal for you to *start* thinking about forgiving the person that hurt you. You may not need to look too far. A good place to start could be your family. How many marriages, friendships and families could be *restored* just by making the decision to forgive? It is *easier* said than done, but one thing is for sure, *it can be done with love.*

I know many individuals in holding cells with a *desire* for someone to forgive them. How wonderful will it be to *stop* and make a *call*, or walk into the next room and *say* to another, "I need to forgive you because I love you?"

Think again and *make that move*, because you could be a part of a *movement* that starts in your *home*, then spreads in your *neighborhood* and then extends across this *nation*.

*We could stomp out racism and hatred.*

"Judge not, and ye shall not be judged: condemn not, and ye shall not be condemned: forgive, and ye shall be forgiven," (Luke 6:37).

# Chapter 2

# True Forgiveness

*Take the first step.*

Life can be *complicated*. Challenges come *each* day. However, living with the richness that peace gives us is without question a far *better* way to live. When you have *truly* forgiven someone in your heart, you will know it for sure.

You may be asking, "Where do I start on my journey to forgive someone?"

Why not start with your heart; *the place where you were hurt*. That is the *first* step. "Heart surgery" is major, but the end results will be *rewarding* in the long run. Do not *lose* hope.

You may be dealing with unforgiveness in your heart. Forgiveness is a *process*. You have the heart to forgive, but you are struggling with the first step.

*Please do not lose hope.*

If you truly seek God with your *whole* heart, He will *help you* move forward. The good news for you is, *it can happen.*

You may be a *believer*. Or you may be an unbeliever, someone who has never *received* or *confessed* The Lord Jesus

20

Christ as your Lord and Savior. If so, it is *important* for you to know that Jesus Christ died for *you*. You can have *eternal* life through Him; by *acknowledging* and *repenting* of your sins, by *accepting* His Love in your heart and by *asking* Jesus Christ to be Lord of your life.

Accepting Jesus Christ in your life will open a *deeper* understanding of God's Love for you. Accepting Jesus Christ as Lord of your life is a powerful step in *empowering* you to move forward in Forgiveness.

## The Answer Only You Know

Only you can answer the question of *why* you are not willing to let go and forgive. The only hurt that Christ's Love *cannot* heal is the hurt you are *not willing to release* to Him. Many are unable to receive healing in their hearts by God's Power because they are not willing to let go and trust God.

Take God at His Word. The prodigal son's father was *ready* and *willing* to let go of the hurt his son caused him. That made it possible for him to forgive his son without explanation. The father's reaction represents God's heart toward us. God *restores* and *reinstates* us when we turn back to Him.

My journey began with a divorce notice from my wife.

She did not ask me if I *wanted* to divorce her. I think she knew what the answer would have been. I did not know how *ready* I was to forgive *without explanation* until my former wife asked me for a divorce. I had already *positioned* myself in life to walk in Forgiveness. Forgiving someone does not *eliminate* the consequences of what you are facing. You still have to deal with the *aftermath* of their actions. When she stated she wanted to divorce me, I did not ask her for the reason. She began to tell me *why*.

How was I able to forgive my former wife even after *she asked me* for a divorce? How was I able to leave *without a thought* of where I was going? At that particular time, I did not have anywhere to go. I believe my time in God's Word *prepared* me for the plight. It was a dilemma I *had* to brave, yet it was a predicament I was *not ready* to face.

The prodigal son's desire to leave probably caught his father off guard. The request must have *hurt*. He probably was not *expecting* his son to leave, let alone *demanding* his inheritance. According to tradition, he was to *receive* his inheritance *after* the death of his father. Instead, what his son's request signified was the *death* of their relationship. In his son's eyes, *he was as good as dead*.

The following week, I started seeking help to face the unwelcome changes that were invading my life.

Divorce Care was a 13-week course that offered someone in my situation help to go through the difficult time. I was so *determined* to not go through a divorce again, so I took the course *five* times and became a *support* to the hurting.

Many shared their stories with me, and what stood out to me was many were still harboring *anger* and *unforgiveness* in their heart from their second or third or fourth marriage. As for me, I had two marriages and two divorces in my past. I begin to pray and ask God to help me so that I would not have the *same* story over and over again.

I asked those who were going through the course once again a particular question. After asking each one the *same question* and getting the *same response,* I wanted an explanation as to *what* happened and *why* after going through the same course they seemed to *perpetuate* the same cycle.

*It all came down to the need for a mindset change.*

If you are a believer, but you are still not *willing* to forgive, *you need to do some soul searching.* The Bible tells the story of ten virgins who *waited* for an invitation from the bridegroom to his wedding feast. Of the ten, five were *invited* in. Five were not, because they did not have any oil in their lamps. (See Matthew 25.) That oil represents a personal and ongoing *relationship* with Christ.

## Check The Oil In Your Lamp.

Scripture teaches us the importance of a *deeper* relationship with Christ that will bring change in our lives. "Therefore if any man be in Christ, he is a new creature: old things are passed away; behold, all things are become new.," (2 Corinthians 5:17).

We can begin to see how much He loves and has forgiven us so many times over in our own life. The Word teaches us to forgive. *The goodness of God leads to repentance.* "Or despisest thou the riches of His goodness and forbearance and longsuffering; not knowing that the goodness of God leadeth thee to repentance?" (Roman 2:4).

When I look at my life and *how much* God loves and has forgiven me time and time again, it teaches me *the importance of Forgiveness.*

When I study about the prodigal son and his relationship with his family, it reminds me of many episodes in my own life with my three sons and two daughters; and in particular, *my older son.* As I am writing this book, he still harbors unforgiveness toward me. It has been *my prayer* that soon and very soon, before Jesus returns for us, and the heavens open up to receive us, *he will forgive me.* I have forgiven him and moved on with my life.

## The Prodigal Son's Brother

The prodigal son's return *uncovered*, what I call, a nest of *unforgiveness* and *bitterness.* His elder brother heard of his return and celebration, but *refused* to join the festivities. You would think he would be *excited* that the family was reunited and that his father was pleased.

Keep in mind, that even *within your own family*, there are ongoing issues. Envy, jealousy, strife, discontent, to name a few. I am sure you can add to the list. Do not be surprised when you see a few folks that are *not excited* about your comeback and restoration. What they have decided to hold on to within their hearts, is keeping them *unwilling* to forgive and let go of past hurts. They would prefer to see you *suffer* a while *longer* or for your struggles to be *perpetuated.* I wonder how they determine whether your trial has or has not lasted long enough.

The elder brother *chose* to observe the festivities from a *distance*. His father came out to *invite* him to the celebration. This was the *second* time the father came out. The *first* time he came out was to meet his *wayward* brother, and now he stood inviting his elder son to come in and celebrate with them.

The elder son could not imagine how his father could forgive his brother so *quickly*, and *without explanation*. The elder son recounted how he had been serving his father *faithfully* all these years, yet his father had *never* thrown a party for him and his friends. The elder son did not know the heart of his father.

## Do You Know The Heart of The Father?

Many of us live life on the *outside* looking in, just like the elder son. Many do not know the heart of God. Many do not know how much God *loves* us, how much He *wants* us to succeed in life and how much He *desires* for us to have joy unspeakable.

The elder brother could not *understand* why his brother had been forgiven so *quickly* after spending his *whole* inheritance. He was *suspicious* of his brother and what he wanted; maybe *more* money...or should we say, *"only"* money *to perpetuate his riotous lifestyle.*

*A selfish heart cannot discern a move of God in someone's life.* The prodigal son's return and celebration *exposed* the elder brother's *true* heart. The elder son never *really knew* his father's heart, because the father had to declare to him, "Everything I have is yours."

There is no record that the elder son ever came to the party to celebrate with his family. Instead, the elder son wanted an explanation of *why* and *what* happened with his younger brother's inheritance; and then maybe, and only then, would he *release* Forgiveness. Your hurt may be so profound that you *require* something *more* before you can forgive. You set up parameters, rules and regulations for restoration and healing; but as soon as that line is *crossed* the door of hurt swings open again.

While pastoring for over twenty years of my life, I met so many believers that found it *hard* to forgive and let go of what someone may have said to them. They continued to *harbor* the pain of that hurt.

It is important to *pursue* a better understanding of the meaning of Forgiveness and why it is important to *forgive* someone and *rebuild* that trust again. Do not *leave* your destiny in the hands of *others* determining if you have suffered long enough. Do not let your restoration follow the timetable in their heart and mind.

*Spending time in God's Word will change your thinking and understanding.* "Be ye angry, and sin not: let not the sun go down upon your wrath," (Ephesians 4:26). "Let the words of my mouth, and the meditation of my heart, be acceptable in Thy sight, O Lord, my Strength, and my Redeemer," (Psalms 19:14).

# Chapter 3

# The Unknown Becoming Known

*My ex-wife was hurting.*

I discovered she needed *out* of the marriage. *The unknown became known.* It was here we started the journey to *resolve* our union of matrimony because she was determined to end it.

All trust was *gone*. When she *admitted* her regret for marrying me, it occurred to me that she *never* actually believed in our union. If we *both* believed in our marriage, I am convinced our marriage would have *survived* and we would be *together* today.

I am writing this book to give you *hope* that you can make it through the pain and disappointments of life. You can come out *victorious*. Forgiving someone and believing in them again will begin the *process* of rebuilding trust.

## Definition of Trust

a) assured reliance on the character, ability, strength, or truth of someone or something

b) one in which confidence is placed. (/www.merriam-webster.com/thesaurus/trust)

Trust is something that is *restored* over time. It may take a *season* to rebuild that confidence. Regaining trust will require *time* and *effort* from both individuals, even after they have forgiven each other.

Time is a *limited* resource. Time is not promised to everyone. God gives you 24 hours each day. Use it to *restore* a broken relationship. You may not have the opportunity to restore that relationship tomorrow.

As you go through the process of rebuilding trust, do not keep bringing up the past every time that person makes a mistake. I would rather see someone *struggling* out of a dilemma and making an *effort* to *change* their behavior, especially if I am walking beside them; than to see them not putting forth any effort at all.

## Who Have You Lost?

The prodigal son's father was *ready* to celebrate as soon as he saw that his son had changed. Have you *discarded* someone special because you looked at them and the situation through the eyes of *hurt*, instead of through the lenses of Grace and Love?

As a pastor, it is easy to *offend* someone without knowing it. Those in your household, who intimately know you, can *destroy* you if the Love of God does not reign in their hearts. This is because they often look at you through the eyes of *the past*. Your mate might expect you to be *perfect*; to never fail or come up short in life. I remember the jobs I worked, and the ones from which I was laid off of, while married to my last wife. I lived under *constant mental stress*, hoping the jobs

I was on would work out and that I would not experience another layoff. Who you *choose* as a spouse matters. Your *success* in life will *depend* on it. Are you on the *same* page when it comes to your relationship with Christ?

This is an important scripture to follow *early* on in your relationship. "Be ye not unequally yoked together with unbelievers: for what fellowship hath righteousness with unrighteousness? And what communion hath light with darkness?" (2 Corinthians 6:14).

Your work will be a big part of what is affecting your marriage. If someone is *making an effort* to get a job, they are not sitting around the house all day playing video games and watching TV; their *temporary* unemployment should not be a reason to not believe in them.

Even after going through layoffs, I would make the effort to get another position. As I look back, I know some of the jobs I did were just a "band-aid" to help me *discover* what I wanted to do in life.

## Be Courageous

The prodigal son had to *encourage* himself to go home.

It is a blessing when someone has the *courage* to ask someone they hurt to forgive them. Once you ask someone to forgive you, give that person *time* to *rebuild* their trust in you. Seek out *godly* counsel. They can work out a strategy that *enables* both of you to move forward.

True Forgiveness is when you are *ready* to love someone *again*. You are the *only one* who can determine why you are not willing to let go and forgive. The *only* hurt that Christ's Love cannot heal, is the hurt you are *not willing* to let go of. The Power of God cannot heal your heart unless *you are ready to let go*.

The prodigal son's father was *willing* to let go and forgive. The father's heart represents God's heart toward us. Having a *deeper* relationship with Christ and *understanding* what He requires of us, is what is missing in many estranged relationships. Only then will you begin to see how much He *loves* you and has *forgiven* you many times over in life. That should teach you to forgive as well.

# Chapter 4

# Dealing With Hurt?

# You Need Help

*What will it take for you to forgive another?*

It is my hope this book will help if you are hurting and give you *clear direction* on what you need to do next so you can be on the road to recovery.

We will start with a *combination of events.* A combination of qualities and decisions that need to be working together in your life at all times to *unlock* God's best.

*Faith – Love – Joy – Forgiveness – Peace – Forbearance – Longsuffering – Kindness – Gentleness – Honesty - Goodness – Meekness – Temperance – Patience.*

## What's Your Combination?

"But the fruit of the Spirit is love, joy, peace, longsuffering, gentleness, goodness, faith, Meekness, temperance: against such there is no law," (Galatians 5:22-23).

Love — Joy

Peace — Longsuffering

Gentleness — Goodness

Faith — Meekness

Temperance

This image illustrates the combination of events that need to take place in our hearts *at all times* to unlock God's very best when needed. Only God's Power can unlock what has been secured in our hearts.

Take a look at this scripture. "If ye be willing and obedient, ye shall eat the good of the land," (Isaiah 1:19). This verse is very clear on what it will take to see God's very best. A willingness to obey God *in every area of your life* will make you free indeed and give you the freedom to live.

"If the Son therefore shall make you free, ye shall be free indeed," (John 8:36). This resonates in my heart because *I am free indeed.*

You can be free as well...*and free indeed*; because that is God's plan for you and the one you need to forgive.

You may be thinking, "I am just not willing to walk in Forgiveness or even apply these steps."

Just finishing this book can help you *prepare* and be *ready* to take the course of action necessary to forgive, to be *free* and to know that *life can go on.*

## You Can Develop This Attribute

Forbearance is defined as the *quality* of someone who is patient and *able to deal* with a difficult person or situation *without becoming angry.*

"We then that are strong ought to bear the infirmities of the weak, and not to please ourselves," (Romans 15:1).

"I can do all things through Christ which strengtheneth me," (Philippians 4:13).

Living in forbearance will *challenge* you because that means you must be willing to live life *without* anger, even when you feel you have been *pushed* to the point of no return.

You might say, "I deserve to be angry."

Even though you feel you have a *right* to be angry, I hope you will not take action to physically and/or mentally hurt someone; which in turn physically and mentally *hurts you.* Get counseling from someone who is capable of helping you *move forward* and *cross over* into Forgiveness.

If we could only come to the place of Forgiveness, I believe we would not see *divorce* rates so high, friends having a *falling out*, brothers and sisters in The Body of Christ *not speaking to one another* and *division* among family members. I will not leave church leadership out of the mix, especially where it applies to pastors and sheep that have left their fold.

*It is time for a reset.*

You may be hurting *deeply* and are *desperately* looking for answers. If you are expecting any changes in your life, it is time you *reset* your priorities.

## It Is Time For Inventory Control

I remember a pastor I sat under years ago. His wife was an excellent teacher. At the beginning of each year, she would do a series on *inventory control*. She would encourage us to check for *overstock*; things we had not let go from the prior year.

*Why not consider asking God to search your heart to see if you have created a backlog of overdue love for someone because you have not forgiven them.*

"Search me, O God, and know my heart: try me, and know my thoughts: And see if there be any wicked way in me, and lead me in the way everlasting," (Psalm 139:23-24).

God's Love is capable of *searching* us and *revealing* what steps we need to take to be *free*.

*You will never really know real freedom until you have forgiven someone.*

*You are never truly living until you forgive from the depth of your heart.*

I remember sitting in on a teaching one afternoon at three o'clock. The pastor's subject was, "Forgiving Someone." He was a man *before* his time. His questions were thought-provoking and challenging.

He had such a Love for The Body of Christ. He was known for *always bringing people together*. I remember sitting in his office and hearing him talk about how hard it was for believers to forgive.

I did not come into a better understanding of what he meant until I became a pastor and faced the "Demas" he often talked and shared about. "For Demas hath forsaken me, having loved this present world, and is departed unto Thessalonica; Crescens to Galatia, Titus unto Dalmatia," (2 Timothy 4:10).

It is time for us all to reset *before Christ returns*. It is time for us to walk in *Love* and *Forgiveness* for one another. We rely on *our strength* to make it each day, yet God is willing to and capable of *helping us* to bear with each other.

## How To Save A Relationship

The key to *saving* your marriage or even a relationship with a family member or a friend is *not giving up* on that person. It can be *difficult* dealing with others and their failures in life, but The Bible is very clear about *bearing one another's burdens and walking in Love.*

"Charity suffereth long, and is kind; charity envieth not; charity vaunteth not itself, is not puffed up...Beareth all things, believeth all things, hopeth all things, endureth all things," (1 Corinthians 13:4,7.) "Brethren, if a man be overtaken in a fault, ye which are spiritual, restore such an one in the spirit of meekness; considering thyself, lest thou also be tempted. Bear ye one another's burdens, and so fulfil the law of Christ," (Galatians 6:1-2).

You can *recover* from adultery. It will take God's Love to help you through that level of hurt. *You can recover.* Betrayal is *hurtful* and any diseases that are a consequence of that indiscretion can be *overbearing.* Just remember, Forgiveness does not *eliminate* the physical or mental impact of the sin. *You can recover.*

Divorce does not need to be a part of your equation to *solve* your problems. Divorce can be *avoided* if you choose to *forgive,* to *face* the issues and *deal* with them now. Break any cycles from the past that may be *impacting* your marriage.

## Restoration Happens When We Forgive

Oftentimes, we are *blinded* because of pride. God's Word teaches us that pride *comes before a fall.* (See Proverbs 16:18).

I was married *twice*, and during each marriage, I *served in church leadership.* That was a train wreck waiting to happen. Two of the ministries were started *in my home*; Trinity Outreach Family Church and Harvest Church. I even served in one other church, Greater Love Baptist Church, after I was voted in by the pulpit committee.

I had many friends, and I also had many enemies. I even had people that were *disappointed* in me. I had a *fight* on my hands just to survive each week.

## A Shout-Out To Committed Friends

It was not until after I started Harvest Church that God sent me what I called *real* and *committed* friends; those who would *stick* with me through thick and thin. This was where I experienced the Love of God through *Forgiveness* and *support*. They loved me so much and they *refused* to choose sides on any matter. Through my relationship with them, I learned the different levels of friendship.

My devoted friends showed up and stood with me to the very end. Elder Andre and Jacquelyn William and Sis Stephanie Williams were troopers. *People I could count on.* Sister Patricia Hayes and her grandkids and Mother Nora Jackson stuck with me no matter how things looked.

The individuals I just mentioned were *faithful* and *unchanging* in their relationship with me. When I was *down and out*, I could always count on them to *help me up*. That is why you need people of *strength* who will not change on you during the difficult times of your life. I will always be grateful and thankful for their *steadfast* and *godly* friendship.

It is important to have friends that will not always *agree* with you; rather they will *always tell you the truth*. It was their *uncompromising* friendship that helped me to be *clear* in my thinking and to look at *both* sides of every argument.

Though they loved my former wife, she did not *receive* their Love for her. She did not *develop* the relationship I had with them. She *misunderstood* their commitment to us and their role in our life, in our ministry and in The Body of Christ.

Those friends remained *faithful* to the calling. I saw in them how *quick* they were to forgive and to *serve* with Love and a genuine heart. I noticed that I did not see the qualities of Forgiveness and friendship in everyone. That was when I realized that people will always make their commitments in relationships at *different* levels.

Yes, I had other friends in the Harvest Church Family, but when everything fell apart, I needed a *greater* level of engagement and assistance. My devoted friends *showed up* and *stood* with me to the very end. Sister Stephanie was a committed and dedicated friend, someone I could count on. Sister Patricia Hayes and her grandkids showed me much love and support. Mother Nora was truly the mother I needed during that season and still is today. Elder Andre and Jacquelyn William, my first life coaches, were sources of strength and instruments of God's unfailing love. Their support for me never wavered. I will always be *grateful* and *thankful* for their friendship.

At Harvest Church, there was a young man that many did not like because of his relationship with one of the believers. I believe he *loved* me and had a heart of *repentance*. He wanted to do the *right* things. To him I say, "Thanks and if I am guilty of anything when it comes to love, I forgive quickly."

I sincerely wanted to have a testimony of *never walking away* from the ministry. I was willing to go on and *keep fighting* the fight of faith. I knew that through all of the darkness and affliction I was going through, if I was going to live and see God's wonder-working Grace and Power in my life, *forgiving* someone and everyone had to be *on the top of my list*.

I am where I am today because of a *forgiving* heart.

# Chapter 5

# Forgiving

*Forgiving someone can be a struggle.*

Forgiving somebody who has hurt you at the core of your soul may be a *challenge*, but it will be *beneficial* in the long run. Having talked to so many hurting individuals over the past few years, I have noticed the same response each time. "I am just not able to forgive because the hurt is deep. You do not understand the pain. I am not willing to let go."

The sad thing about *withholding* Forgiveness from another is, that person will continue along the *same* direction without changing. When our children *hear* us say we are unwilling to forgive someone for the wrong they committed, we are subconsciously *teaching them not to forgive* those who have done them a disservice.

I have heard some individuals say, "I can forgive them for what they did to me but not for how they hurt our children." This is where the seed is *planted* in them not to forgive. That may be the reason why so many fathers do not have a *relationship* with their children today.

Every new year starts with a *new* commitment to change. When I read the statements of changes many were willing to make for a *better* life, I never saw Forgiveness on the top of any list.

If you are not a believer and you are struggling with forgiving someone, I want you to know it will never happen until you are willing to let go of the pain. Jesus Christ can help you *let go* of the pain. Jesus Christ can help you see *victory* and *live again*.

You may be a leader in The Body of Christ and the church *hurt* you. You may be a pastor, who had a brother, or sister in The Lord, *wound* you; yet you thought they were *truly* your friend. Please do not allow that to *cloud* your view of the True and Living God Who *loves* you.

So many, believers and unbelievers alike, are *harboring* pain in their hearts. Unforgiveness could be the reason the scripture teaches us that in the last days there would be *a great falling away*. (See 2 Thessalonians 2:2-3.)

## Guard Your Heart

It is important for you to have a *personal* relationship with Jesus Christ as your Savior. Having an *intimate* connection with Christ will keep you from *falling away* and from *blaming Christ* for any hurt. Many blame God for the pain in their life, because the enemy *blinds* them to His Love for them. You can break *free* today. Know that God *loves* you and *did not cause* your hurt.

As you start on the path of Forgiveness, know in your heart and mind that God will *help* you do what you cannot do *on your own*. I cannot begin to *overemphasize* the power of forgiving someone. Take the time to let that person *know* you have forgiven them. For the process of *rebuilding* trust to begin, you must both come to an *agreement* as to what *needs* to be in place to help restore *confidence* in the relationship.

God's Word is very *clear* about obedience; the *willingness* to obey and the *benefits* you receive because you did. This verse explains it well. "If ye be willing and obedient, ye shall eat the good of the land: But if ye refuse and rebel, ye shall be devoured with the sword: for the mouth of the Lord hath spoken it," (Isaiah 1:19-20).

## Heal Our Land

Israel had a *history* of rebelling against God's plan for them. God used kings like Nebuchadnezzar to come in and take over their land. Their *captivity* was a result of their rebellion. The Bible makes it clear what God will do if we would only *obey Him corporately*.

"If My people, which are called by My name, shall humble themselves, and pray, and seek My face, and turn from their wicked ways; then will I hear from heaven, and will forgive their sin, and will heal their land," (2 Chronicles 7:14).

It is time for the land to *heal* and *change* for the best so we all can live in *harmony*. Can you imagine how life could be if we would all forgive each other quickly? Imagine how much better society would be if we would let go of the past?

Sunday Morning is the *most segregated* time of the week, yet heaven will be populated by believers from *every race*. True Love and Commitment starts on this side of life...from this side of eternity...*while we are still alive on planet Earth*. True Love and Commitment starts with *forgiving* one another and choosing to live in *harmony*.

God's Word says the only way they will know us is by *the love we have for each other.* "By this shall all men know that ye are My disciples, if ye have love one to another," (John 13:35).

That is something the enemy of our soul does not want to see manifest, *nevertheless I believe it will happen before Christ returns.* "That He might present it to Himself a glorious church, not having spot, or wrinkle, or any such thing; but that it should be holy and without blemish," (Ephesians 5:27).

# Chapter 6

# Be True To Your Commitment To Forgive

*Make a commitment to forgive.*

Having a *strong* commitment to forgive will set you *free*. The very moment you decide that you are *ready* to forgive that person for the hurt that caused you an insurmountable season of pain is the moment you *start* to live again. Moving forward will *lift* a load of pain off of you because you were never designed to *carry* this weight in your heart.

I attended the funeral today of someone I did not know personally. I *knew* her brother. The speaker spoke *well* of her. He shared with everyone how *forgiving* she was. It was *encouraging* to hear that she had a forgiving heart.

I could not help but wonder how many were sitting there in attendance hoping they had a chance to *ask* her to forgive them. That was surely not the time to *ponder* those thoughts. All that musing would do is bring guilt and pain. If there is anything you will get from this book, please do not *wait* until it is *too late* to ask someone *to forgive you* or for you to tell someone *you have forgiven them*.

How blessed are we when we see someone that brings *hope* and *strength*, and not the spirit of *division*? "Blessed be he that cometh in the name of the Lord: we have blessed you out of the house of the Lord," (Psalm 118:26).

# Be Wary of The Spirit of Division

The spirit of division will *keep* you on the same cycle of *discord*. The spirit of division will drive a *wedge* between the person you are trying to reconcile with and yourself. The spirit of division will *prevent* you from finding a place of healing.

You have an enemy that wants to *hinder* you from *advancing* in your relationship and moving *forward* with your life. If you could only see the *flaws* of holding on to hurt and the *unfruitfulness* of harboring bitterness.

I would not want to leave the earth having *held* unforgiveness in my heart *against* someone, knowing it could have set them *free*. It is time to *wake up,* because we are being *robbed* of God's best.

Unfortunately, that is the reason many *hop* from church to church; but find *no hope.* Looking for the answer, but seeing *no results.* Many end up *discouraged*, thinking it is *useless* to proceed. If they knew how *close* they were to the solution, they would *not give up.*

*All they need to do is walk in Forgiveness.*

Doubt only creates *more* doubt. If you are dealing with unbelief, resolve to *fight* through it. Walk with a forgiving spirit. Do not allow any unforgiving spirit to *control* your life.

Become the kind of person that *builds others up* by teaching them the importance of forgiving one another. That could be the *vehicle* God will use to *stop* the next divorce from happening.

## You Can Be The Solution

I mentioned earlier about the person who left a legacy of forgiving others quickly and not harboring bitterness in her heart. Do you know anybody that may be angry at another? Maybe *you* can help that person. They may have a *problem* with their pastor. You just might *prevent* them from *hopping* from church to church, looking for answers that are not forthcoming, because of the issues *within* their own heart.

Scripture reveals that in the last days there will be a great *falling away*; and that is something you and I see coming to pass *each day*. (See 2 Thessalonians 2:2-3.) As believers, our job is to *pour healing oil* on the hearts of those that truly have a heart's desire to *change* and to be *restored* to their rightful place.

Remember the prodigal son? He had a *change* of heart because of the *insurmountable* problems he was facing. He set his heart to come home to what he already had *before* he left. He did not *recognize* what he had at the time, just like so many that fail to see the *benefit* of keeping their marriage away from the divorce court.

How many hurting people *desire* to be restored, yet are walking in *fear* because of the track record of the *rejection* they received from others? The prodigal son *knew* he would be *received* and his father would forgive him.

How many people in your life, *know you will forgive them*? Maybe this is the very area of your life you are *struggling* with. You have a *hard* time forgiving others. They *know* you very well. How wonderful would it be if you were to turn over a new leaf, *communicate* your Forgiveness to them and *welcome* them back into your life?

Keep in mind this may not work in *every* circumstance because of abuse or physical hurt. Please know it is not God's plan nor His will for you to live in an *abusive* situation that will cause *harm* to your *life*. God did not *ordain* some marriages that have gone to divorce court, but that does not mean they could not have been *turned around* and *saved*.

Unless we come to a place of repentance and are restored, many will stand before Christ and will not be prepared to not hear Him say, "Well done, thou good and faithful servant...enter thou into the joy of thy Lord." (See Matthew 25:21.)

You must be *willing* to forgive. God can help you to have the *strength* to forgive and move forward with your life.

*Forgiving is living.*

When you forgive, you *acknowledge* you experienced hurt. You have made the decision that the pain, injury and damage done to you in the *past*, will not continue to *define* you in the *present* and in the *future*.

# Chapter 7
# Healing In Your Body And Mind Starts With Forgiving

*Forgiveness is a healer.*

God has an *expectation* of us. You cannot *expect* to get heaven's pardon if you are *not willing* to look past some earthly offenses. "And when ye stand praying, forgive, if ye have ought against any: that your Father also which is in heaven may forgive you your trespasses," (Mark 11:25).

This scripture reveals what *forgiving* someone will do for you and for the one who *offended* you. This verse keeps me *motivated* to keep my heart *clear* of any ill feeling toward anyone that has wronged me.

It happened on New Year's Day in 2015 at 10 am. That's the moment my ex-wife *asked* me for a *divorce* and for me to move *out* of our home.

*That day I had an out of body experience.*

I remember standing *outside* my body looking at the both of us, as my former wife stood there *explaining* to me why she no longer loved me.  She said to me that she *regretted* the day she married me.

I had to *shift* from my hurt and my feelings and rely upon the Lord's *word* that was in my heart.  I *knew* we were having *problems* in our relationship.  I felt that any suggestions I would have made to *remedy* the relationship were out of reach.

Trusting God to do what I could not was imperative.  Remember, your will is *yours* and you can *override* God's purpose for your destiny.

My ex-wife did not ask me if I *wanted* the divorce.  She *knew* what my response would be.  Instead, she said, "I want a divorce!  Here is the paperwork.  All I need you to do is sign the dotted line!"  I could not believe what I was hearing.

She put the paperwork in my hands and told me the divorce will be *final* in 30 days.  I was looking at myself and yelling hysterically at the same time, "Please do not sign the papers!"

## What Happens Next?

The next thing I knew I was back in my body looking down at the papers.  Many things were going through my mind at that very moment.  One thing I knew was I was not going to sign anything without *praying* it through and *hearing* from God on the matter.

Relieved and not feeling the *pain* that caused the out of body experience, I said to her, "Listen, I really need some time to think about this before signing the papers."

I could not believe *what* was happening to us and *why* it was happening.  All I knew, I was back in my body and I needed to somehow pull myself together.

I gathered up the few belongings that I could at the time.  I did not know where I was going to spend that night or where I would live.

# I Was Hurt

My ex-wife did not make the transition any easier, because she was on the phone *laughing* with someone.  I thought to myself, "You just asked me for a divorce, and here you are laughing on the phone?"

As I stood there looking at her, it was like I had just stepped into a *whirlwind*.  It seemed I could not get any air in my lungs.  I felt like someone had just *dropped* a ton of bricks on my chest, and here I was, *pinned* on the floor by the weight of them, *unable* to breathe.

*I loved her.*

I did not want it to be *over*.

I just could not believe the woman I loved *no longer* loved me.  The one thing she had *at the top* of her New Year resolution list was to make sure to *start* the first day of 2015 with me *signing divorce papers.*

As all these thoughts were going through my mind, I knew a big part of my healing was going to start with forgiving her; *that very moment and time.*

My mind was moving at the speed of light. I needed to forgive her *promptly* if I was going to have a chance of living and moving forward with my life. I forgave her *that* day; *before* I left our home. That was not as easy as simply slapping anointing oil on my forehead.

## She Will Not Take Advantage of Me

I had to get to a place where I could *think clearly*. Even though I was *devastated*, Mark 11:25 was operating in my heart. I had to *heal* from the shock of what was happening between us. I needed to forgive *quickly*, because I did not need my body to break down.

This book is all about Forgiveness and my *experience* of living by faith. I had nothing to prove. I had Jesus in my heart. God is faithful to *keep* us and *protect* us even when things are *falling apart* in our life. Somehow, I knew God was going to *use* what was happening to me to *heal* others as I shared with them this message of Forgiveness.

It took a season for me to get where I am today. It is my hope that I can *help* someone to heal and to know that life is *worth* living. I loved her *immensely*. I did not think I could *recover* and be the man I am today. After reading an article by Cynthia McGee on Emasculation, I now understand what I was dealing with and why I felt the way I did, "BUT GOD."

## Your Body Is Talking To You

You need to *listen*, because your body is *hurting*.

Forgiving someone who has hurt you is extremely *beneficial;* opening the door to better *health* and *well-being.*

Forgiveness is what you need to *live* your life again.

Once you realize what is *keeping* you from moving forward, you will no longer *fake* it just to go through the motions each day. May the light switch turn on and may you *realize* that unforgiveness is making you sick; only *delaying* your healing.

You can stand in *hundreds* of prayer lines, but until you forgive, you will *never* experience the life God has for you.

You will never be *totally* free.

I know that is *hard*, but it is the *truth*. You need to *stop* listening to someone's opinion and *gather* the facts for yourself. What will it take to move *undoubtedly* forward in life with God's Abundance and Love spreading all over the world? *Forgiveness!*

## Leave Your Gift At The Altar

God instructed you to *leave* your gift at the altar and *get things right* with anyone you have a dispute with. "Leave there thy gift before the altar, and go thy way; first, be reconciled to thy brother, and then come and offer thy gift," (Matthew 5:24).

Until you come to this realization, you will not *enjoy* the abundant life God is calling you to on this side of heaven. May you not stand before God in the days to come without *truly* finding a place of repentance and getting things *right* in your life.

You may have been taking all kinds of medication, but it has not worked, because you are still feeling the pain. Could it be that *releasing* Forgiveness on someone's life is the right "pill" that will *heal* you of what is *making* you sick?

# Chapter 8

# Is Your Will His Will?

*Your decisions start with your will.*

Bad decisions are the reason why we are in *trouble* today. God sent His Son to *restore* what we lost in The Garden, the day man used his will to *disobey* God and act *contrary* to His command.

*Why do we struggle to do what is right in life?*

*Why do we have so many problems with our will?*

To *answer* that question, we must first look to God's Word for a *deeper understanding* of the will and *why* it gets us in trouble. God sent the Last Adam to *restore* what the first Adam failed to do.

"And so it is written, The first man Adam was made a living soul; the last Adam was made a quickening spirit. Howbeit that was not first which is spiritual, but that which is natural; and afterward that which is spiritual. The first man is of the earth, earthy: the Second Man is the Lord from heaven," (1 Corinthians 15:45-47).

*Jesus restored it all to us.*

When my last wife asked me for a divorce, I responded that it was *not* God's Will. She replied that she believed God gave her the *okay* to divorce me, even though The Bible reveals God *hates* divorce.

"For I hate divorce!" says the Lord, the God of Israel. "To divorce your wife is to overwhelm her with cruelty," says the Lord of Heaven's Armies. "So guard your heart; do not be unfaithful to your wife," (Malachi 2:16 NLT).

I *concluded* it was *her* will to divorce, so I *accommodated* her desire. According to that scripture, we are *both* wrong for going ahead with it.

The "pill" I took for the divorce was 1 John 1:9 that states, "If we confess our sins, He is faithful and just to forgive us our sins, and to cleanse us from all unrighteousness."

Thank You, Jesus, for *forgiving* us and *healing* my heart. I pray the same for my former wife.

*God gives you the power to make decisions on your own.* It was *never* His will for you to be a *robot.* Making a decision *without* consulting God can be *devastating* to your future. Look at me. I have been *married* twice; and I have *divorced* twice. Some would say, "twice the fool."

*I have learned my lesson.*

Each day, I am learning what it means to *truly* trust God with my life. It took me 61 years to learn this, but I feel more *alive* today than I have for a long time.

How do you *change* your will to God's Will?

*Obedience!*

"If ye be willing and obedient, ye shall eat the good of the land: But if ye refuse and rebel, ye shall be devoured with the sword: for the mouth of the Lord hath spoken it," (Isaiah 1:19-20 KJV).

## 5 Willingness Principles To Remember

1. You must be willing to *change.*
2. You must be willing to *extend love.*
3. You must be willing to *forgive those that hurt you.*
4. You must be willing to *set others free.*
5. You must be willing to *let go to be free.*

The more time you spend in God's word, the more it will *build* your faith, give you the *ability* to obey His every word, and *grow* you to perfection and maturity.

*Your will will become His Will.*

# Chapter 9

# Could It Have Been ED

# of The Mind?

*Something was not right.*

I was in a *dysfunctional* marriage for 17 years. It finally came to light on the 1st of January at 10 am. That is the day everything became clear to me to as to why I had *erectile* dysfunction. If I could get a dollar for all the red flags I *noticed* in our relationship, I would be a *rich* man today. I even recall sharing with my former wife that I kept *expecting* her to ask me to *leave* and she kept insisting it was not true.

That fateful morning, my former wife walked into the dining room and *asked* me for a divorce. It happened at the same table *we ate on*...the very table on which *we prayed with each other*...the actual table *we played games with our friends* whenever we invited them over.

It was a table the two of us had selected...*together*.

She never *asked* me if *I wanted to divorce her*. I really do not think she ever *loved* me. She was a *wonderful* woman and I *loved* her immensely. It took me *two years to heal* from the hurt. I *commend* her for staying in the marriage and all that time giving me what I thought we had, when in reality it was an illusion of *hopelessness* for her when she eventually got to the place where she knew it was not going to work out.

## She Was Willing To Speak Up...

I applaud her for having the *courage* to state the truth of what was really in her heart, even though it meant we would never be together again. I still believe God would have *intervened* on our behalf if we would have come into *agreement* and *trusted* God to do what needed to be done.

Her forthright statement shed light on why I dealt with erectile dysfunction during our marriage. She claimed that for seventeen years she had lived with the *regret* of being married to me. She alleged I was *not* capable of taking care of our family, even though I was a *working* man. She stated that I *never* met the needs of our household per her expectations.

I would like to believe we had intimate moments in our marriage when things did *click*, because the morning after she would *thank* me for the night before. I would look back at her and think to myself, "For real?" I had very little confidence when it came to making love to her, even though I loved her.

Remember, by her own admission in asking me for a divorce, she stated how she *regretted* the *entire* seventeen years of marriage. Think about this. How many marriages are spent in *regret*, and the *only* way they know to *solve* the problem is through *divorce*. Believe me, that is not the answer. If I recall correctly, she did ask me for a divorce once before, but we worked *through* it and decided to stay *together*.

Many marriage issues in America can experience a powerful change when we *truly*, and in a *loving* way, *forgive* each other.  For seventeen years, I *struggled* with performance issues.  I cannot begin to count the doctors I talked to during that time; and the tests and procedures that were done to *cure* my problem.

## A Myriad of Doctor Visits

My doctor visits were about *improving* and *helping* my performance.  The doctors would prescribe Viagra, Levitra, and even Cialis to help me.  All they did was gave me terrible headaches.  The next step was the needle, but it never did happen; and I am very *thankful* I did not go through with it.

I must have visited and talked with *everyone* I could think of for help; who was an *expert* on the subject of erectile dysfunction.  I read *every* article I could on the subject.  I began to think I was a *lost* cause.  I began to accept this was my *plight* in life.

## Walking In Forgiveness Was My Only Option

I looked for *different* ways to *show* I loved her; by *serving* her and openly showing her how much I *cared*.  A day did not pass without me *reading* God's Word and other literature on the subject.  I did not want anything coming *between* us. I would ask God to *search* my heart to make sure I was not walking in a spirit of unforgiveness.  I had to keep myself *encouraged* in The Lord, *daily*, because I really *wanted* our marriage to work.

I knew how she felt about me as a pastor.  I was not helping her spiritually.  As far as she was concerned, my messages were not helping anyone else for that matter.  This is where I really *learned* how to walk in Forgiveness and Love.

*I knew my responsibility as a Pastor.*

This is why it was so hard for me to understand why so many believers around me could not forgive others and move on from the offense. By God's Grace and Love, I needed to walk in Forgiveness every day.

When I look back at my life, I know my doctors were *God-sent*. Each doctor would have the *same* report; there was *nothing* wrong with me. Each doctor would tell me over and over again that I did *not* have a problem. All my tests would come back, and the reports were *always* the same. The doctors confirmed that I did not have an issue with low-T. I never had to *struggle* to rise to the occasion. My cholesterol levels were *ideal*. I had no *blockage* in my blood vessels.

I was a *healthy* man with *normal* testosterone levels.

However, even with all these *positive* reports, I still remained *unconvinced*. I wondered if something was *wrong* with the water system in our home. I remember reading one particular article that stated plastic bottles would *affect* a man's testosterone levels.

## "You Do Not Have A Problem!"

Every time I visited my doctors, they would give me the same *positive* report and *reassurance* over and over again that I did not have any medical issues. They tried to help me *understand* that I did not have a problem.

These doctors did not *know* each other, yet they all came back with the *same* result. They were *right* in their diagnosis, but I was *not* convinced. They sensed my *agony*, so they offered me the *leading* pills they had on the market.

I told one of the doctors I was seeing at the time that I wanted to look *elsewhere*. I was considering going to Boston Medical Group. He urged me not to go, *assuring* me there was nothing wrong with me. He even *warned* that going would probably create a problem for me. I am so *thankful* I did not go.

## Listen To Your Body

Your body will *speak* to you. All you need to do is *listen*. Your body will never *lie* to you. My body was *telling* me what was wrong with me, but I would *not* listen. I kept *declaring* to my body that it was *sick*; yet my body kept *revealing* to me it was not being *loved* by me or by my wife.

Whatever you are saying to each other may be *killing* you both. Your words need to *change*. Be *courageous*. Make the *right* moves for your marriage to *survive*.

While I was consulting with the doctors, I felt so downcast that I *considered* asking my first wife what she thought of me as a lover. I did not have the nerve because she was *re-married* at the time.

I craved a *solution* to my dilemma.

I have great respect for one of my doctors in New Orleans. I visited him for four years while we were living there. Every time I went to see him, I discussed my performance issues. He alerted me that the issue was not with me and may be with *my wife*. My response was that all she needed to do was lay there. He laughed and said the issue was deeper than that.

## There Is Hope For Your Marriage

Perhaps you are *struggling* with what I was dealing with. Maybe you are *looking* for answers because of your *inability* to perform in the bedroom and make love to your wife. Conceivably you may be wondering why a *single* pill will not help you with the issue the two of you are facing together.

*As long as the two of you stand together, there is hope.*

Unless it is an *abusive* marriage, divorce is not the answer. Divorce is something God does not *tolerate* nor *desire* for either person.

Be *honest* with yourself.

Ask yourself if the reason you are *struggling* with forgiving your husband or your wife is because of some real hurt that cut *deep* into your heart; such that when you touch each other, the fire is *gone*. If both parties are in *agreement* and *want* the marriage to work, the answer you need can come through counseling.

*God wants your marriage to work for both of you.*

You can both come back *stronger*. Divorce need not be an option. Divorce is not something to be *trifled* with. I would not want anyone to go through that type of pain. I went through it *twice*. It was not a pretty picture.

That is probably why I am *cautious* about moving forward with marriage again. Your whole life can be turned upside down if love is *one-sided*; it will affect your *well-being* and *performance* in life and marriage.

## Uncovering Our Intimacy Issues

That morning, when she asked me for a divorce the second time, the muddy picture of our life together became *clearer*. After seventeen years, she *admitted* that marrying me was a *mistake*. It became *evident* to me she *never* loved me. That was why we had *intimacy* issues all those years. I went back to thank my doctors for all they did to try and convince me it was not me physically, *but mentally*.

*Would you want to be married for convenience?*

Would you go through with a marriage to *avoid loneliness?* Do you want someone in your life so badly, you are willing to do *anything*; even if it means marrying someone *you do not love?*

You may be asking why it took her so long to make up her mind that she no longer wanted to be married to me?

*That is a question only she can answer.*

## Reading The Signs

The truth of matter was, there were red flags all over our life and marriage. I was not the man she *needed* or even *believed* in. I *fervently* prayed that I could be that man.

*She never once acknowledged me as her man.*

She never *validated* me or gave me evidence to know that I was her man. When I asked her why she never *encouraged* me or *assured* me of who I was to her, she responded by saying that was what she did for her father and she was not going to do that for me. That was when I should have known I was *not* the one for her.

*She would never affirm me.*

Stop looking for help in all the *wrong* places. Did you reach for a pill? Or maybe you went for the needle? *Stop!* Take a step back. Do a heart and soul inventory.

Be honest with *yourself.*

Sometimes, because of pride, you both may not be willing to *admit* you have a problem. You end up going through life *unfulfilled*; refusing to deal with the elephant in the room. How do you deal with the elephant in the room?

*A bite at a time.*

I still *believe* that Love is on the horizon for me. This is my Declaration of Faith for *my future wife.*

> *I'm looking for that special Love that*
> *Will hear my heart skip a beat...someone*
> *That's ready to be loved in a real*
> *Way that will change her life*
> *Forever... I'm looking for that*
> *Kindred spirit... I want her*
> *To know that I can love her*
> *In my mind and heart... I want her*
> *To know that I can love her*
> *So much that she can even*
> *Trust my mind because my thoughts*

*Donald W Smith*

*Will only be on her... A man that*
*Can protect his mind can love*
*For real... I'm that man, I've done it*
*Before and I'm looking to do it again*
*But this time with someone*
*That will truly love me...*

# Chapter 10

# My First Marriage

*Did I learn anything from my first divorce?*

You may be wondering why I would go through a *second* divorce if I learned anything from my first marriage? The answer is obvious. *I did not.* Why? Here I was *again.*

Linda, my first wife, was a lovely woman. The first thing I noticed about her was her eyes. She gave me some attention. My first marriage failures *spilled* over into my second marriage. That may have happened to you as well. You may be in your second or third marriage; and you feel some *discontent* in your heart.

This is a good time to do some *soul searching.*

You may be asking, what do I mean by soul searching? Any time you deal with your soul, remember your *will* has a lot to do with it as well. Are you still harboring *hurt* from your *last* marriage? Is there anyone you have not yet forgiven?

This is a good time to get things *right* and *close* that chapter; so your *present* marriage can have a *chance.* I remember having nightmares from my first marriage *several months into my second marriage.*

I recall driving back to Fort Worth after a T. D. Jakes Men's Conference. I stopped by Linda's house to see my children. I stood on the front porch, in front of everyone who was sitting there, including her husband, *and asked her to forgive me.*

You might say that was *brave*, but I would say it was *liberating*. You might be wondering how her new husband *reacted* when he heard me asking her for Forgiveness. He was a *great* man with a *noble* heart and for that I will *always* be thankful. I have a lot of *respect* for him. He was also a *friend* and a wonderful *father* to my children; and for that I am extremely *grateful.*

At the time of writing this book, he had passed away and my *only* regret was never telling him how much I respected him. My former wife's second marriage was *excellent.* She was *happy* and I was happy for her.

After asking her to forgive me, *I never had another nightmare.* Your former wife or husband may have married and moved on with their life. Trust God to give you a *strategy.* You may not have a front porch opportunity like I did, but *God will provide a way* if that is something you *desire.*

"For if ye forgive men their trespasses, your heavenly Father will also forgive you: But if ye forgive not men their trespasses, neither will your Father forgive your trespasses," (Matthew 6:14-15).

# Chapter 11

# My Second Marriage

Spine (Definition): a). A series of vertebrae extending from the skull to the small of the back, enclosing the spinal cord and providing support for the thorax, abdomen and backbone. b). The part of a book's jacket or cover that encloses the page-fastening part and usually faces outwards on a shelf. (Complete Online Oxford 11 Dictionary.)

Spine (Definition): a). Something resembling a spinal column or constituting a central axis or support. b). The part of a book to which pages are attached and on the cover of which usually appear the title and author's and publisher's names. (Merriam-Webster's Collegiate Dictionary: Eleventh Edition Online.)

Stay with me. I am going somewhere with this and it will be clear by time you get to the *end* of this chapter. I heard from my Graphics Artist concerning the problems he was having adjusting my book cover to Amazon's specifications and procedures. I had *already* turned everything in and purchased the ISBN (International Standard Book Number) for my book. He informed me that I would not be able to *display* the title on the spine. That only confirmed to me that I was *not finished* with my book.

The spinal cord *supports* the backbone. I needed to have the backbone and courage to *write* about my second marriage. I needed to *press* toward the mark of the high calling of Christ Jesus with the help of The Holy Spirit. The real test was in *truly* moving on; and to my amazement, today I am *healed* and *delivered* to the glory to God.

## Lady of My Dreams

While I was in my *last* marriage, I truly *believed* I was *in* the will of God and was married to the lady of my dreams. To be truthful, I kept seeing red flags throughout our marriage. I *applaud* her for hanging in there with me for as long as she did. What *courage* and *grace* it must have taken for her to *stay* married for as long as she did to someone she was not happy being with. If you are married to someone you are not happy with, please pray and ask The Lord to *heal* your heart and help you to *save* your marriage.

I remember talking with someone who had been *married* four times and was currently going through her fourth *divorce*. I was interviewing her for my book and was asking some tough questions about why she thought she found herself in the same place again. I was essentially in the same place as her.

## Learn From Past Experiences

You may be asking why I would be *qualified* to ask questions concerning a *failed* marriage. Unless you learn from history, divorce will *continue* to be a go-to place when you are unhappy and believe that the *only* answer to your problem is *another* termination.

You too may *know* the pain of divorce. You may have been the *victim* and took the *brunt* of the pain. I can remember proudly describing my marriage, as a carousel with happy music and smiles; not knowing what was coming down the road for us. Yet, my ex-wife was *well* prepared when she gave me the news that she wanted *out* of our marriage.

Needless to say, I was not. The reality of it all hit! This did not fare well for my ego. I was facing *another* divorce. My life had come to a *drastic* stop. I embarked on some *deep* soul searching. Here I was now having to *vacate* the home we had shared for many years.

She made it very clear she did not want me to have anything to do with the home, because in her mind she did *everything* and I was only a spectator, who did not make any contribution. To this day, I am not sure where my paychecks went. However, now it is time for me to smile.

I loved her *immensely*. I *wanted* the marriage to work. I was *faithful* in every way; even in mind and will. I did not *want* anyone else, even *after* we were separated. It has been three years since our separation and divorce. I have been living single, and I still find it *hard* to move on. Believe me, I have not remained single because I am still holding on for her to come back. That is not going to happen nor do I want it to happen.

I do commend her, because she hung in there for 17 years. I would like to think, maybe it was the love I had for her that *kept* us moving and maybe she *hoped* one day to love me as much as I loved her. At times, I can still hear her saying,

"I regret the day I married you." Those words are like a ringing in my ear. I am sure with time, *that too will pass*.

## Moving Forward

I hope only the *best* for her. I hope the next time around she is more than just *happy*, but also *fulfilled* in every way and the love she had for God is *prevalent* again in her life.

Perhaps you are still in your *first* marriage and you are *contemplating* a divorce because you believe that is the only *answer* to your happiness. At this point in your life, having the *right* individuals around you is so *important*. You do not need people that will agree with you. Instead you need people who will help you to think a lot *clearer* before you make a decision you cannot *reverse*. You need people around you who will *help* you *find* your way.

I noticed how my wife had started to *change* whenever she became a part of a running group. She became *distant*. I realized later that I was only praying *against* her will, because she had *other* plans; and that was to go on with her life *without* me, no matter what.

## God Did Not Fail Us

I want to make sure you know that God did not forsake us. I need to *emphasize* that one thing is for sure, God was *in* our lives and *wanted* us to make it. God is not the author of confusion. "For God is not the Author of confusion, but of peace, as in all churches of the saints," (1 Corinthians 14:33).

This next verse is very *clear* on what will happen if we line our will up with God's Will for our life. "If ye be willing and obedient, ye shall eat the good of the land," (Isaiah 1: 19).

God will never *force* us against our will to obey Him. For there to be *success*, it takes two to *agree* before they can even move forward. "Again I say unto you, That if two of you shall agree on earth as touching anything that they shall ask, it shall be done for them of My Father Which is in heaven," (Matthew 18:19).

She had already decided that being married to me was not an option. Make no mistake about it, even the way I ended up with the divorce papers proves how *serious* she was about *ending* our marriage. I waited as long as I could, hoping against hope, that her heart would *change*.

She knew my schedule very well. I can remember pulling up to my Monday night meeting and noticing an individual who looked like he *needed* help. I appeared to be the only one *willing* to step up to assist him.

When I walked up to him, he *awkwardly* handed me some papers, all the while asking me if he was in the right place. The next thing I knew, he *jumped* into his car, leaving me with the papers that he had *stuffed* in my hands. He almost drove *into* the wall as he was trying to leave.

Crazy me, I stood there thinking, "Why did this guy leave his papers in my hand?" Only after unfolding and reviewing the papers, did I realize I had been *served*. I find some *humor* in what happened that day, because it was *amusing* to see that gentleman trying to drive through the side of a building, just to get away; thinking I was going to be angry and jump on him.  How funny is that?

## Where Are You Now?

Are you *contemplating* divorce?  The sad thing is, your spouse may not even be aware of your intentions.  Now is a good time to do some soul searching.  If you are a believer, ask God to *intervene* and *help* you to have His mind concerning this decision.  Seek counseling.  Please be *prayerful* and *discerning*.

Consulting the *wrong* counselor, who has the wrong *motive* and *intention,* will make it even *worse*.  I have heard devastating accounts of individuals who have been through that.  You do not want anyone to take *advantage* of you both while you are in a *broken* state of mind.

I can remember asking her if she would *consider* counseling.  She initially said she would think about it, but later decided *against* it.  I am sure someone she consulted did not agree with what I wanted for us. That is why you need to make sure you are talking with the *right* individuals.

If you are experiencing *physical harm* at the hands of your spouse, you need to *get out now*; because it is not the will of God for someone to *abuse* you.

## What Did I See In Her?

The thought has probably crossed your mind.  What did I ever see in her that got my attention?  Her relationship with God.  I was willing to do whatever it took to get with her with the hope of us becoming more than friends and more like husband and wife.

The question is, "Was I fully healed from my first divorce?" Looking back now, I can give you a resounding, "No!" I was *not fully healed* and I was definitely *not ready* for matrimony again. She too had probably not fully healed from her *prior* marriage.

I want to make sure this is clearly understood. I was her *third* husband. She had been single for a while. When we got together, she was just coming out of a *difficult* break up. I can remember being told, "I can do bad all by myself!"

*Is that how you feel now?* Please do not give up on your marriage because you do not love someone or you may find yourself moving in a *wrong* direction in life.

Love is not a feeling; *love is an action.*

So many couples marry for the *wrong* reason. It should not be that way, because doing so can *destroy* someone's life. That is *wrong* on many levels, especially with regard to *honoring* God and His Word. At the time, I *believed* God had put us *together*.

Now, after three years since my divorce, I have finally come to the realization that God did not put us together. Yet, He would have *helped* us stay *together* and *find* love in each other. Believe me, I have struggled with believing that was the case, but the evidence keeps showing me I was *wrong* when I *initially* married her.

# Seek The Lord

You are probably at a *crossroads*, thinking there is no hope for me. Do not stop *looking* for hope. Do not give up on your marriage. I am not trying to give you *false* hope. However, if you are both on *talking* terms and can find a place of *agreement*, especially if you are both believers in Christ, you have a *responsibility* to seek The Lord.

If you can, find a place of *hope* you both can *agree* upon, and *work* from that place. Remember, God *hates* divorce. Even if you married for the *wrong* reason, ask your spouse to *forgive* you. *Repent* and ask God to forgive you as well. God will take you both from that place of *hurt* and heal your *hearts*. You both can have a testimony of God's faithfulness to *restore* when you truly *trusted* Him.

This book is about *forgiving* someone. If you are not a believer in Jesus Christ, know that He is *willing* and *able* to *help* you as well. Accept Jesus in your heart and watch how The Lord will take *charge* of your life and *heal* you of the brokenness in your heart.

Once you *accept* Jesus Christ in your heart, it is important that you *find* a body of believers. Grow as a disciple of Christ. This is the road you are on now. In this book, I map out the plan of salvation, with you *accepting* The Lord Jesus Christ into your heart. However, your journey does not end there. You need to be around *other* believers of like faith to help you *grow* in Christ and if you would like to email me please do so. My email address is on the last page of this book. I can help you further in your journey to know Christ in an even *deeper* way.

I have written enough about my second marriage and it is my intent that this book will give you *hope* and *direction* from this day forward. Divorce is *painful* and it affects so many areas of your life. It is my hope to help you *avoid* the pain. I have gone through it *twice*. My goodness, did I learn anything? I believe I did.

# Chapter 12

# Loving Someone While Married

In this chapter, I will share with you my definition of love, straight from my heart; my perspective of *being in love* with who you are married to.

Over the years, I have learned, that to *truly* love someone, you must be *ready* to forgive *at all times*. You are loving an *imperfect* person. You are saying that no matter what happens, despite the *mistakes* and *failures* that you both will make and experience, you will face them *together*; in the good times and in the bad. One thing is for sure, *you can make it!*

One day after our church service, someone made a comment to me that he noticed how *longsuffering* I was with others and with him as well. My two *failed* marriages would probably reveal I was not longsuffering, but I like to think that was not the case.

My second wife *claimed* I did not treat her at home the *same* way I treated her in public. I kept *wondering* what kind of a man I was, because of the picture that was being painted of me. People *believed* her. After watching an episode of Dr. Jekyll and Mr. Hyde, I almost believed it myself. Maybe I was *different* at home in a way I did not know.  I *loved* her.  Each day I treated her with *kindness*.  What you saw in public, I assure you, was the *same* at home.

People would say to me, "Well, you know how people are in public.  They are not the same behind closed doors."  If you believe that to be *true*, then your understanding about people is way off the mark.  You *cannot* put everyone in the *same* category.  It may be true in *some* cases, but not so with everyone.

I am so thankful I do not prejudge people that way.  As you are reading this book, you know where I am coming from.  Have you ever been *accused* of being something you were not?

## Have You Ever Been Misjudged?

I remember looking at the church family during that time and observing how everyone was looking back at me.  Believe me, it was *painful*.  With every step I took, it became *harder* to breathe.  I was hurting all over my body.  It was like being *pinned* to the floor with a ton of bricks resting on my chest.

I could do nothing but *love* and *forgive*, while being misjudged at a level I could not even put into words.  I learned how to forgive and walk in love *at all times*.  I kept my focus on The Lord and His Love for me.

*The Lord's loving hand preserved me.*

The Power of God's Love kept me going.  l would like to *thank* those that loved me *unselfishly* and were carriers of God's Grace into my life.  I *appreciate* them for standing with me, praying for me and putting money in my hand. When I was *down* to nothing, God was always up to *something*. His Love kept me *encouraged* when I was at the point of not knowing if I could take another step.

"O taste and see that the Lord is good: blessed is the man that trusteth in Him," (Psalm 34:8).

## Another Definition of Love

The definition of love is not giving up on someone. God does not want us to give up on each other. Instead, He desires for us to *love, forgive* and *trust* His Provision. The father kept hope *alive* because each day he *looked* for his son to return. (See Luke 15: 11-23.) When his son finally returned, he *forgave* him without explanation and *restored* him back to his *rightful* place. The question remains, *are you willing to do the same?*

"And he arose, and came to his father. But when he was yet a great way off, his father saw him, and had compassion, and ran, and fell on his neck, and kissed him," (Luke 15:20).

I have pastored *three* ministries. Pastoring with a spouse who is not on the same page is a *challenge*. If you are both in ministry, and you both feel like giving up, please do not. I would encourage you both to find a way to *refresh* yourselves, because ministry will *drain* you if you do not take a break and *rebuild* your strength.

Dear Minister, you need a break. If you do not take one, you may *regret* it later. The church is not your *bride*. You are their *undershepherd*. Back to back, for a couple of years, we took a break and cruised the seas; and it appeared that everything was going well for us and for the ministry. However, that did not help us *resolve* our issues. Yet, at the time I really thought it did.

Communication is the *key* to discovering the *hidden* areas of pain in each other's lives. Find a place of *refuge* and start *freely* communicating with your spouse. If you do not, it may *hurt* your ministry. God knows I do not want what happened to me to transpire in another ministry. It is not worth it.

If there is anything I can do to *encourage* you, please do not hesitate to email me. It is hard for a pastor to *trust* someone else with their *deep* hurt. My email address is on the last page of this book. I promise to respond to you. God has a *friend* on this side of heaven who will be a *true* friend to you.

## The Goodness of God

"Or despisest thou the riches of His goodness and forbearance and longsuffering; not knowing that the goodness of God leadeth to repentance," (Roman 2:4).

Let that last verse *soak* in your heart. The goodness of God *leads* to repentance. One strong belief I have in my heart is, many believers *struggle* with forgiving someone; because, for some reason, they have *forgotten* how much God *loves* us and *expects* us to love our brothers and sisters. A husband and his wife must be *quick* to forgive and *commit* to loving each other *unselfishly*.

God has a *standard* to which we should all press toward. "Then came Peter to Him, and said, Lord, how oft shall my brother sin against me, and I forgive him? Till seven times? Jesus saith unto him, I say not unto thee, Until seven times; but, Until seventy times seven," (Matthew 18: 21-22).

You could say, "I can do bad all by myself." Sometimes you feel alone because of the *insurmountable* problems that have *ravaged* your life. Remember, God *loves* you and will *help* you. He will *empower* you to do the *right* thing in someone's life if you *truly* desire that in your heart.

# Chapter 13

# Longsuffering Is
# The Order

*Your marriage is worth saving.*

As I look back over my past and *examine* the blueprint of my life, I must say longsuffering was a *vital* component. All through my second marriage, I kept *hoping* that things would *change*. I did not know the pressure I was under until I was driving *away* from the house; the day she asked me for the divorce. Even though I had forgiven her, that did not *appease* the hurt I was feeling at the time.

The change I was believing for did not happen. If anything, the complete *opposite* occurred. God's Love could have saved us both the heartache and pain of a divorce; but He needed *two* parties to be *willing* to be obedient to His Word. There were times when my former wife and I did not agree on something, so she would surmise we needed to *agree to disagree*.

That is the exact opposite of *scriptural agreement*.

We should have stood on Matthew 18:19; "Again I say unto you, That if two of you shall agree on earth as touching anything that they shall ask, it shall be done for them of My Father Which is in heaven."

God would have *healed* our relationship if we could have come into agreement. My hope for you is that you can find a *place of agreement* with your wife, your husband, your family member, or even your boss; so you can experience the *victory* and *harmony* you desire.

Longsuffering is the order. Longsuffering does not imply you will *fail* in what you are believing and trusting God to do. This book was written so you can *learn* from my failure. I would not want my *worst* enemy to go through what I have gone through.

## God's Plan For Your Life

What I went through was *never* God's plan for my former wife's life or for my life. God's character is about *Forgiveness* and *restoration* of battered lives; for those who are *willing* to be obedient. "If ye be willing and obedient, ye shall eat the good of the land," (Isaiah 1:19).

I kept *hoping* change would come in my marriage. You may be hoping for the same to happen for you. May the message in this book help turn things around in your life. May you do what I could not do; *convince* your spouse that the marriage is *worth saving*.

*Your marriage is worth saving.*

Muster up the courage to talk with the *right* people, those that *believe* in you and your wife. Longsuffering is the order. God's grace can help you in this season.

As I drove away from our home, I wanted to turn the car around and say to her, "Let's fight a little harder. Let's find help." However, I knew she had already made up her mind to move on; and indeed, she had.

God did not fail us. *We failed God.*

It was never His plan for us to divorce each other, even though I had no choice but to go along with it. "With all lowliness and meekness, with longsuffering, forbearing one another in love," (Ephesians 4:2).

## Your Marriage Affects More Than Just You

Marriage problems do not only affect homes; they also affect *churches, businesses, schools* and *neighborhoods.* Over the years, I have worked for various companies and had numerous conversations with business owners and managers from different parts of society.

I recall working with a business owner in New Orleans. I walked into his office one day and saw that he had set up a bed in his warehouse. I thought that was strange. He saw the look on my face, so he began to explain that he and his wife were *separated* and were now going through a divorce. The only way he could *save* his business and *keep it going* was to live *on* the premises. He shared with me what happened and how he was feeling at the time. I have not seen him since I moved from that great state. However, I think about him often and wonder how things turned out for him.

When a business or marriage begins to fail, *separation* happens because someone is not only *hurt*, but may also have trouble *forgiving* the other and moving *forward.*

I know too well how it is when you sit across the table from someone, be it in business or in marriage; and you declare, "I am with you. I will support the vision. I will be here for you when you need me. I am all in!" Only to discover later that those words were worthless.

*They did not mean it.*

## Are You Being Fed?

I pastored what some would call a *small* flock of believers. I was challenged in many ways, but one thing was for sure; *forgiving* had to be on the top of my list. I worked at all levels in that church, especially with my former wife.

I remember asking her if she *listened* to any of the messages that I preached and taught. Her response was that she was not listening and *no one else was.* I could not believe it, but I knew it was true. She claimed I was *not helping her* spiritually.

I said to her, "Your spiritual growth is more important than this ministry. Why don't you find a ministry you can go to and be fed, because your relationship with Christ is more important than being with me."

*Believe me, that was hard to say.*

This was difficult for me. I ran to God and cried out to Him to *help* me to forgive. My hope was that what I was going through would not *affect* the ministry. I *quickly* forgave her and preached *every* Sunday, knowing *she did not care for my message.*

You might think it strange, but I *thank* God, I went through that season. That experience pushed me *closer* to Christ. When the day finally came that she asked me for a divorce, and wanted me out the house, I was *spiritually* prepared for it. I had formed the habit of *relying* on His Love for me. Did it make my experience any easier? Absolutely not! *It made it bearable.*

Only a pastor will understand, that when you mount the pulpit, with the hopes of pulling someone out of their pit in life, that your *unsupportive* wife can be a *challenge.* I call that preaching *in* season and *out* of season. I had a lot of *out of seasons* as she sat on the front row. She was the *mirror* of our home.

## Do Not Cause Deeper Hurt

You may be a pastor's wife who has chosen *not* to support your husband because you have unforgiveness in your heart. He may have unforgiveness in his heart toward you. May God help you both, because so many are walking through life with an *unforgiving* spirit. You may have *deep* hurts and find it *hard to forgive* your husband. You may be *contemplating* divorce to hurt him, based upon how you yourself *are* hurting or have *been* hurt.

*Please! Make an effort to save your marriage!*

Do not take it to a place where it may cause *deeper* hurt among the people you *love* and *serve.* Ask God to *help* you *forgive* him, so both of you can *heal.* If that does not happen, your divorce could *destroy* your ministry. I am speaking from experience, because so many believers were *hurt* as a result of my divorce. Even though we know divorce is not easy, there should be a way to *ease* the pain.

*Fight for your marriage!*

If you see no other way out but divorce, do not *destroy* your spouse in the process. This is the time to *seek* The Lord and make sure He is part of the progression of your decisions.

You may be a pastor *contemplating* divorce. It is not worth it. The pain will be *unbearable*. It will *affect* the flock God entrusted you with. I live with the *failure* of my ministry each day. The Body of Christ was hurt *deeply*.

## Your Forgiveness Will Inspire Others

Forgiving each other will *teach* others and give *hope* to marriages in The Body of Christ. Someone is saying, "If the pastor cannot make it, I know we cannot. He is supposed to be closer to God." *You do not know how many times I have heard that quote.*

My wife did not leave the ministry *decently and in order*. (See 1 Corinthians 14:40.) You may ask, how can you divorce decently and in order? If questions are not answered in the way others can *understand* them, then the pain they feel as a result of your divorce will go *unanswered*.

If my former wife would have *stood* before the believers and *said* something, I would not have appeared like Dr. Jekyll and Mr. Hyde. Her *departure* from the church was not something I could *recover* from, because the congregation *struggled* with believing if I was truly what I said I was.

At the end, there was a remnant that *stuck* by me and *wanted* me to be healed. When it was all said, and done, I wanted to have a testimony that I did not walk away from the ministry. That is something I will *always* be *thankful* for.

You may be a pastor who is *struggling* with forgiving someone. You may even have unforgiveness toward me, *for not standing with you during tough times*. It is time to *clear* the air and get things *right* before Christ returns. Many pastors are walking in unforgiveness because of hurt from the leaders who surrounded them; *elders, deacons* and *musicians*.

I had leaders in the ministry who were *constantly* late to services and meetings. That was an *indication* to me that they were leaving and would not be with me for long. I had this one minister who would not give until the church service was *over*. I always wondered why he always had to go to the ATM to *complete* his giving. I never asked why. I was *longsuffering* with so many. I hoped *change* would come. I loved them immensely, because I truly want to hear God say to me, "Well done thou good and faithful servant." (See Matthew 25.)

It may be hard to believe you can *truly* walk in this area of Forgiveness. The reason for that is a lack of *understanding* of God's Word. It is time to *find* that person you need to forgive; by phone, by text, by email, or even by knocking on their door.

# Restaurant "My Beloved"

I received a letter from an incredible lady, my former wife and I met in New Orleans, while serving at a particular ministry. She *commended* us on the *example* we set and how she was *encouraged* for what The Lord would do for her as well. She *appreciated* the love I had for my wife.

While we were married, we received many *accolades* from couples who *testified* that we had set a beautiful example of *Love* and *Commitment*. However, when I look back, it was an *undercurrent* of the disaster that would soon happen.

We went as far as bringing couples into our home. We would set up a cafe called *Restaurant "My Beloved."* We would have dinner and an incredible time of building *healthy* marriages. We decorated it to create a *fun* and *loving* atmosphere and served non-alcoholic beverages. It was my hope that our relationship would be a *shining* example of what marriage should be; *yet we failed miserably.*

I thank God for the couples that joined us. They set an impressive example of Love and Commitment before us; and always kept me *encouraged* in The Lord. I love them immensely and will never forget how they *affected* my life during my time of healing and how I received *strength* from them to *stand firm.*

On the next few pages, I share images from Restaurant "My Beloved" and of a couple that joined us at one of our events.

Restaurant "My Beloved"

My beloved is mine, and I am his, Who is delighting among the lilies. SS 2:16

# Letter of Appreciation

Here are the words from a letter written to my wife and I when we served together at one of the churches.

*Hi Rev and Ms Smith,*

*I am writing you these few lines to let you know that I am having a wonderful time and that I am getting plenty of rest. I would also like to take the time to thank you both for being a part of Vacation Bible School. If F.P.B.C had just a few more dedicated, determined and in love with Christ Christians like the two of you, our youth department would be awesome.*

*Please continue to pray for me that one day I can stand before a group of people and really speak for God. See, I know what I want to say and I know what is in my heart; but God has been so good to me and my family that I can't tell it without shedding tears of joy.*

*Gina, you are so truly blessed to have a husband who is so much in love with you, and Rev Smith, you are blessed for having a wife and kids like you have. I know your marriage is not perfect, but believe me, it is one that a lot of people wish and pray for.*

*I enjoy and admire both of you, and I want to let you know that I am so very, very, very glad that God directed you to join with us at First Pilgrim and to work in the Youth Department. I thank God for you both.*

*Well, I am going to close now because my daughter will be back soon and I do not know what she has planned for me, but I could just stay right here in this beautiful home and enjoy this peace and quiet, but she likes to take me places so I'll see you Saturday, June 26th.*

> *Love you both,*
> *Sis Pat.*

## Please Forgive Us

I want to reach out to you, The Body of Christ, and ask for you to *forgive* my former wife and I, because we did not *manage* our marriage properly, in *keeping* our wedding vows.

God's Word *commands* us to *love* one another and to *forgive.* We needed to set the *example* that God *expected* of us. I *failed* in both my marriages. Many of us, as leaders, are quick to say, "We are human."

I would agree, *but that is no excuse.* I have had men of the cloth tell me, "Why didn't you just divorce her and marry someone else?"

I am so glad I did not listen to that advice. I did not pull that card, because God's Word is very *straightforward* on the *standard* we needed to set. I am so glad I listened to *godly* men that gave me counsel *according to God's Word*; and not their opinions. God's Word will *never* fail.

What a *hard* pill for me to swallow once everything was over. Here I was facing the fact that she *never* loved me. If she did, we could have *weathered* the storm and *trusted* God to do what we could not do on our own.

If you are *considering* divorce, even if you may have *already* submitted your application, please *pray* and get the mind of The Lord before making a *huge* mistake and *destroying* someone's life; especially if they are *willing* to *fight* for the marriage.

## We Shall All Stand Before God

Please remember, one day, *all of us will stand before God*. It will be good to set the record straight *before* that happens. In some cases, your marriage may be completely over because they have already married someone else and there is no chance for reconciliation.

Set the record *straight* on this side of heaven. *Repent*. Ask each other for Forgiveness. Stop listening to someone casually saying, "It is going to be okay." Read God's Word for *guidance* and *confirmation*.

*Be on your guard*. Do not be *unfaithful*. "'The man who hates and divorces his wife,' says the Lord, the God of Israel, 'does violence to the one he should protect,' says the Lord Almighty," (Malachi 2:16 NIV).

The only One Who can give you hope for tomorrow; that you may *know* He is pleased, *is God Himself*. His Word will *stand* the *test* of time. He will *forgive* you for your failures and will help you live a *victorious* life that will bring Him glory and honor.

Seek godly counsel; not someone's opinion. Be ready to *receive* the truth and do not be easily *offended* by it. Do not be *preoccupied* with having someone agree with you, simply because you want things to go your way *instead* of God's way.

I ask each of you in The Body of Christ to forgive my former wife and I. Know that the service I rendered to each of you was *real* and *authentic* in every way.

# Chapter 14

# What Was I Thinking?

*God was all I had.*

Very few *appreciate* that when pastors and their wives are working *together* in ministry, it is a labor of *love* and *commitment.* I remember the few members that *remained* after news of my divorce became public. By then, many others had already left, and I knew it was not going to be long before the few who remained *departed* as well.

It seemed that the exit door was only swinging *one* way.

I remember when several of those who remained expressed to me that they believed God was leading them to move on. You are probably wondering what I was thinking as all this was happening. I was in the midst of a sure-fire *test* of *forgiving* and *walking* in Love. As several families were about to make their *exit* from the ministry, here I was asking God to keep us *together.*

I appreciate how those that *remained* handled me in their transition. Many just *left* without saying a word, and there were a *few* who informed me of their departure with a text message. Even though it was a gut-wrenching experience, I could not help but think about the many pastors I knew who had endured testing times in their ministry.

By the time members started leaving the church, my former wife had already made her exit. We were going through our divorce. I knew this was just another trial on how I was going to handle forgiving someone. I knew God, yet my character was being *tested*. I knew if I was going to be an *example*, I needed to forgive *quickly*.

You may be a pastor, a co-pastor or a pastor's wife. You may be the leader in a company you started with your spouse. At one point, you believed in each other; but here you are now alone, and your hurt is deep.

## I Have News For You

During this dark time in your life, know that it is going to get *better*, and things will *change*. Even though we may have never met, *I am praying for you*. Even though I may not know you personally, *I want you to make it*.

This is a good time to start over. Make a decision to move *forward*. You do not have to live looking at your life through the eyes of hurt.

After you have been hurt or abandoned, it is hard to trust *again*; especially after you have given so much of your life to the relationship. This is the time to *regroup*. You need to *surround* yourself with real friends who will speak *the truth* to you. Even though it may hurt, it will *uncover* what you need to do to move forward.

Yes, this is a time of *brokenness*. However, I know God will *heal* your heart and walk with you both *through* the storm. If you are facing this season *alone*, with no real support you can count on, then ask God to *bring* new friends into your life.

"The sacrifices of God are a broken spirit; a broken and contrite heart, O God, you will not despise," (Psalm 51:17).

This book is entitled *Forgive Who?* We all know that someone we *need* to forgive. Why not take out a pencil and paper and begin to write down the names of individuals that need *to hear* from you. That is one way to take the pain off of your mind. Get it on a piece of paper so you can start the process of *letting go*.

Forgiving someone who hurt you, letting go and not holding anything in your heart toward them; is *strengthening*, *encouraging* and will *heal* you quickly.

## Who Needs To Hear From You Today?

Even if it is a letter, *that is a start*. That letter may *open* the door of someone's heart to *communication*. I remember working with Kairos Prison Ministry and watching the prisoners reading letters from individuals on our team that spoke to their hurt. Many began to *cry* and *weep*. The pain was so *deep* and they needed to forgive and let go.

You may be a pastor and someone *promised* to walk with you in this season, yet they are *missing* in action. It is time to forgive and let go, so God can bring *new opportunities* into your life.

God has not *forgotten* you.

However, before He can bring a *new* Harvest into your life, you must first *let all of the hurt go* and *forgive* those who promised to stand with you...*but did not.*

A local pastor was encouraged by the leaders in his ministry to *leave* his job. They *promised* to *replace* his salary, and take care of him and his family. Several months after leaving his good paying job, the leaders *left* the ministry without expressing why.

*The pastor was devastated.*

I am pleased to announce, he did make it through the struggle. He *passed* the test. God was *faithful* to bring him out.

## One Phone Call Can Make A Difference

How many relationships with your brothers, your sisters or your family members, who may have caused the pain you are going through; can be *restored* with just *one* phone call? If you are finding it hard to forgive, but you feel something *tugging* at your heart, you need *to make things right.*

If you need some *support* to help you move forward, look at the last page of this book, and you will find my contact information. Please email me your prayer request and I will stand with you through this season of change.

As you begin to think about what you can do to make things right, please consider that your efforts may not be well received. *At least you have done your part.*

The name of this chapter is *What Was I Thinking?* I thought a lot about what I was going through. Going down was painful. Like most men, I was thinking and asking God how I could *fix* this trial I was facing. My reputation was in the gutter. My members believed the latest press releases about me without seeking to *validate* the facts.

The Lord said to me, "Donald, could you fix a person's heart and make them think a certain way?"

I replied, "No! I could not."

## This Is How My Healing Started...

Healing *finally* came for me. God spoke very *plainly* to me that I needed to *trust* Him because *all I had was Him.*

The following verse is very *clear* about how soon we should *start* the process of forgiving someone who has hurt us. Offenses are not *easy* to overlook. That is why you *need* The Lord's help.

"Be ye angry, and sin not: let not the sun go down upon your wrath," (Ephesians 4:26).

If all you have is God, that is *enough.* You may be thinking, "Pastor Donald, I need to know this God that you are talking about. I need to know what my step will be."

Well, the God I serve is *faithful* to *save* and *turn* your life around. By *repenting* of your sins and *asking* Him to be Lord of your life; if you really mean it, you can start a *new* life today!

You may have *whispered* or *recited* prayers before in your life. If you have never prayed the sinner's prayer to *accept* Christ in your heart and *receive* Him as The Lord of your life, *this is your opportunity*.

Pray this prayer below:

"Heavenly Father, in Jesus' Name I repent of my sins and open my heart to let Jesus come inside of me. Jesus, You are my Lord and Savior. I believe You died for my sins and You were raised from the dead with all Power. Fill me with Your Holy Spirit. Thank You, Father, for saving me in Jesus' Name. Amen."

This next verse will help *guide* you in your *new* walk. It is important to find a fellowship of believers, that will help you grow *stronger* and have a *deeper* understanding of what has just happened in your life.

"That if thou shalt confess with thy mouth the Lord Jesus, and shalt believe in thine heart that God hath raised Him from the dead, thou shalt be saved," (Romans 10:9).

"Whosoever therefore shall confess Me before men, him will I confess also before My Father Which is in heaven," (Matthew 10:32).

# Chapter 15
# My Declaration
# of Faith

My *Hope* for Tomorrow!

I still *believe* that Love is on the *horizon* for me.

I want to make sure *everyone* knows I have not given up on loving someone *again*. I am *first* making sure I am *fully* healed. It is my prayer that the person I will meet one day will be completely *honest* with me and be *ready* to join me on this journey of marriage.

On different occasions, I have met *lovely* ladies that *wanted* to be a part of my life. Today, I look back and I know for sure I was not ready. I am *more ready* today than I was then. I *know* in my heart it is *time* to move forward and *find* that special someone.

Someone who is *ready* to be loved. Someone who will *commit* to another who will be committed to her; *faithfully, as unto The Lord*. Below you will find some of the *personal* thoughts I am having of her. We have *not* met yet. However, as I wait, I have written some thoughts from my heart; because my *past* will not determine my *future*.

------------------------------------------------

Being *true* to her before marriage is my *gift* to her; *trusting* God for what is *best* for us, is our gift to *each other*.

---------------------------------------------

I am *looking* for that *special* love that will *hear* my heart skip a beat.

Someone who is *ready* to be loved in a *real* way that will *change* her life forever.

I am *looking* for that *kindred* spirit.

I want her to *know* that I can *love* her in my *mind* and *heart*.

I want her to know that I can love her so much that she can even *trust* my *mind*, because my *thoughts* will *only* be on her.

A man that can *protect* his mind can love for *real*.

I *am* that man.

I have done it *before* and I am looking to do it *again*, but this time with *someone* that will *truly* love me...

---------------------------------------------

I need to be put to *sleep* like Adam; until God *wakes* me up and says, "Here *she* is!"

---------------------------------------------

Sex *outside* of marriage is *not* on my To-Do List.

"But I keep under my body, and bring it into subjection: lest that by any means, when I have preached to others, I myself should be a castaway," (1 Corinthians 9:27).

-------------------------------------------------

My love for her is *safely* tucked away in my heart.

-------------------------------------------------

Don't *stop* believing, Baby.

I just need a little *more* time.

I am *closer* than you think.

"And the Lord God said, It is not good that the man should be alone; I will make him an help meet for him," (Genesis 2:18).

# Chapter 16
# Devotional Scriptures On Forgiving

First, I want to *thank* you for *perusing* this book. I pray that God will *heal* your heart, and like myself, you will *find* your way again. You will grow *stronger*. You will make all your *future* decisions through *prayer*. You will *trust* God.

If you became a believer in Christ because of this book, I pray that the scriptures below will *point* you toward God and create a *burning* desire in your heart to *read* God's Word, *The Bible*. I pray that you will become a *strong* disciple of Jesus Christ and *find* a body of believers who will *encourage* you in your new walk of faith.

If you are someone who walked *away* from Christ, I pray your faith will be *rekindled*, you will *realize* the love He has for you and you will come *back* to Him.

-------------------------------------------------

"Bear with each other and forgive one another if any of you has a grievance against someone. Forgive as the Lord forgave you," (Colossians 3:13 NIV).

"For if you forgive other people when they sin against you, your heavenly Father will also forgive you. But if you do not forgive others their sins, your Father will not forgive your sins," (Matthew 6: 14-15 NIV).

So watch yourselves. "If your brother or sister sins against you, rebuke them; and if they repent, forgive them. Even if they sin against you seven times in a day and seven times come back to you saying 'I repent,' you must forgive them," (Luke 17:3-4 NIV).

"Get rid of all bitterness, rage and anger, brawling and slander, along with every form of malice. Be kind and compassionate to one another, forgiving each other, just as in Christ God forgave you," (Ephesians 4:31-32 NIV).

"If we confess our sins, He is faithful and just and will forgive us our sins and purify us from all unrighteousness," (1 John 1:9 NIV).

"I, even I, am He Who blots out your transgressions, for My own sake, and remembers your sins no more. Review the past for Me, let us argue the matter together; state the case for your innocence," (Isaiah 43:25-26 NIV).

"Repent, then, and turn to God, so that your sins may be wiped out, that times of refreshing may come from the Lord," (Acts 3:19 NIV).

"Come now, let us settle the matter," says the LORD. "Though your sins are like scarlet, they shall be as white as snow; though they are red as crimson, they shall be like wool," (Isaiah 1:18 NIV).

"Therefore if any man *be* in Christ, *he* *is* a new creature: old things are passed away; behold, all things are become new," (2 Corinthians 5:17).

"In Him we have redemption through His blood, the forgiveness of sins, in accordance with the riches of God's grace," (Ephesians 1:7 NIV).

"Then He adds: "Their sins and lawless acts I will remember no more," (Hebrews 10:17 NIV).

"The Lord our God is merciful and forgiving, even though we have rebelled against Him," (Daniel 9:9 NIV).

"For He has rescued us from the dominion of darkness and brought us into the kingdom of the Son He loves, in Whom we have redemption, the forgiveness of sins," (Colossians 1:13-14 NIV).

"...as far as the east is from the west, so far has He removed our transgressions from us," (Psalm 103:12 NIV).

"In accordance with your great love, forgive the sin of these people, just as you have pardoned them from the time they left Egypt until now." The LORD replied, "I have forgiven them, as you asked. Nevertheless, as surely as I live and as surely as the glory of the LORD fills the whole earth," (Numbers 14:19-21 NIV).

"Who is a God like you, Who pardons sin and forgives the transgression of the remnant of His inheritance? You do not stay angry forever but delight to show mercy. You will again have compassion on us; you will tread our sins underfoot and hurl all our iniquities into the depths of the sea," (Micah 7:18-19 NIV).

"This, then, is how you should pray: "'Our Father in heaven, hallowed be Your Name, Your kingdom come, Your will be done, on earth as it is in heaven. Give us today our daily bread. And forgive us our debts, as we also have forgiven our debtors. And lead us not into temptation, but deliver us from the evil one.' For if you forgive other people when they sin against you, your heavenly Father will also forgive you. But if you do not forgive others their sins, your Father will not forgive your sins," (Matthew 6:9-15 NIV).

"And when you stand praying, if you hold anything against anyone, forgive them, so that your Father in heaven may forgive you your sins," (Mark 11:25 NIV).

"This is My blood of the covenant, which is poured out for many for the forgiveness of sins," (Matthew 26:28 NIV).

# Additional Resources

Time For Results Coaching
Donald W. Smith, President
Motto: Intention, Follow Through, Results
Email: *donaldsmithtx@gmail.com*


I highly recommend you contact a DivorceCare group in your area. *www.DivorceCare.org*
(I also offer this class as well. For updates email me.)


Help for battered women:
*www.internationalwomenshouse.org*


Help for battered men (this is no joke):
*www.healthyplace.com/abuse/domestic-violence/battered-men-battered-husbands-its-no-joke/*

# About The Author

Donald W Smith is the President of *Time For Results Coaching* located in Fort Worth, Texas, where he presently resides. He is the Founder and former Senior Pastor of Harvest Church and had the honor of serving his community in that position for over twelve years.

Donald W Smith received his Associate of Arts (A.A.) in Theological and Ministerial Studies from Tyndale Theology Bible College of Fort Worth, Texas. He also received his Master of Divinity (M.Div.) in Theology, Marriage and Family Therapy/Counseling from Christian Bible College of Louisiana in 2002 while he was living in New Orleans.

What he shared in this book is near and dear to his heart; so if this book has helped you in any way, you can reach him directly at: *donaldsmithtx@gmail.com*